FLIGHT

The Journey of Charles Lindbergh

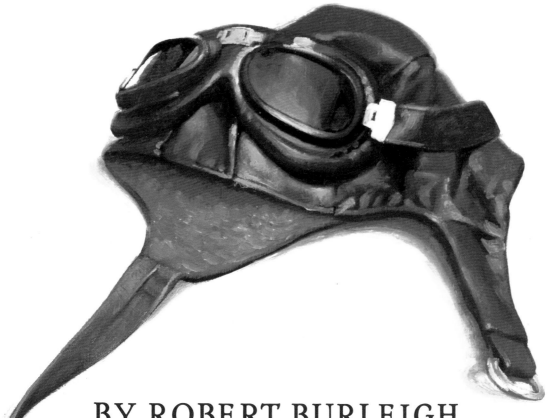

BY ROBERT BURLEIGH

ILLUSTRATED BY
MIKE WIMMER

INTRODUCTION BY JEAN FRITZ

The Putnam & Grosset Group

"A lonely impulse of delight,
Drove to this tumult in the clouds."

W. B. Yeats

To my son, *Elijah Seth Wimmer.*
I hope these illustrations may take
your imagination on a *Flight* through history.

M.W.

Printed on recycled paper

The author would like to gratefully acknowledge Charles Lindbergh's own
The Spirit of St. Louis, *published in 1953, upon which this book was based.*

Text copyright © 1991 by Robert Burleigh. Illustrations copyright © 1991 by Mike Wimmer.
All rights reserved. This book, or parts thereof, may not be reproduced in any form
without permission in writing from the publisher. A PaperStar Book, published in 1997 by
The Putnam & Grosset Group, 200 Madison Avenue, New York, NY 10016.
PaperStar Books and the PaperStar logo are trademarks of The Putnam Berkley Group, Inc.
Originally published in 1991 by Philomel Books. Published simultaneously in Canada.
Printed in the United States of America. Lettering by David Gatti.

Library of Congress Cataloging-in-Publication Data   Burleigh, Robert.   Flight/by Robert Burleigh.   p.   cm.
Summary: Describes how Charles Lindbergh achieved the remarkable feat of flying nonstop and solo from
New York to Paris in 1927.   1. Lindbergh, Charles A. (Charles Augustus), 1902–1974—Juvenile literature.
2. Transatlantic flights—Juvenile literature. [1. Lindbergh, Charles A. (Charles Augustus), 1902–1974. 2. Air
pilots. 3. Transatlantic flights.] I. Title. TL 540.L5B83   1991   629.13′09111–dc20   [92]   90-35401   CIP   AC
ISBN 0-698-11425-6
10 9 8 7 6 5 4

INTRODUCTION

One day when I was a girl living in Shanghai, China, my mother called me into the living room where she was reading the morning paper. "Look at this," she said. "A young American named Charles Lindbergh has just made the first airplane flight across the Atlantic Ocean. Without stopping. And he did it alone." Her tone of voice said, "This is history." Of course it was.

Planes were still such a novelty that when one flew over, people rushed outdoors to see it. There were no commercial planes for carrying passengers and it would be twelve years before a service was started to take people across the Atlantic.

I looked at the picture of Lindbergh. Grinning, with his goggles pushed back on his forehead. He was twenty-five years old, the paper said, and had been flying since he was nineteen—in air shows, as a pilot for an airmail service, and recently as an officer in the Army Air Service Reserves. I grinned back at Charles Lindbergh. Obviously he was the world's hero now.

Mine too.

—Jean Fritz

It is 1927, and his name is Charles Lindbergh.
Later they will call him the Lone Eagle.
Later they will call him Lucky Lindy.
But not now.
Now it is May 20, 1927, and he is standing in the still-dark dawn.
He watches rain drizzle down on the airfield. And on his small airplane.
The airplane has a name painted on its side: *Spirit of St. Louis*.

Lindbergh is nearly as tall as the plane itself.
And yet—he is about to attempt what no one has done before:
To fly—without a stop—from New York to Paris, France.
Over 3,600 miles away.
Across the Atlantic Ocean.
Alone.

He climbs into the boxlike cockpit that will be his only home
    for many, many hours.
He clicks on the engine. He listens as it catches, gurgles, and roars.
A few friends are here to say good-bye.
They are only a few feet away, and yet to Lindbergh how far off they seem.
They look up at him and wave. "Good luck! Keep safe!"

A telephone wire stretches across the far end of the field.

To touch this wire will plunge the plane to the ground.

There is an extra fuel tank in front of the cockpit.

Because of this, Lindbergh cannot see straight ahead.

Will the *Spirit of St. Louis,* with its over 5,000 pounds, rise into the air?

To keep the plane lighter, Lindbergh is leaving behind his radio and parachute.

Will that be enough?

He has been up all night getting ready.

A thought runs back and forth through his mind:

It is still possible to turn back. To return home.

And yet another thought is stronger:

I have been waiting my entire life for this flight.

Lindbergh lowers his goggles and nods his head: "Go!"

Men on each side push to help the plane roll over the soggy ground.

The little plane bumps forward, gaining speed.

The wheels leave the ground, then touch back.

The plane seems to hop, taking its "last bow to earth."

On the third try it stays aloft.

It soars above the wire by only twenty feet.

The *Spirit of St. Louis* rises in the air.

It is 7:52 in the morning, New York time.

Lindbergh points his plane toward the Atlantic and beyond, toward Paris.

Over thirty hours away.

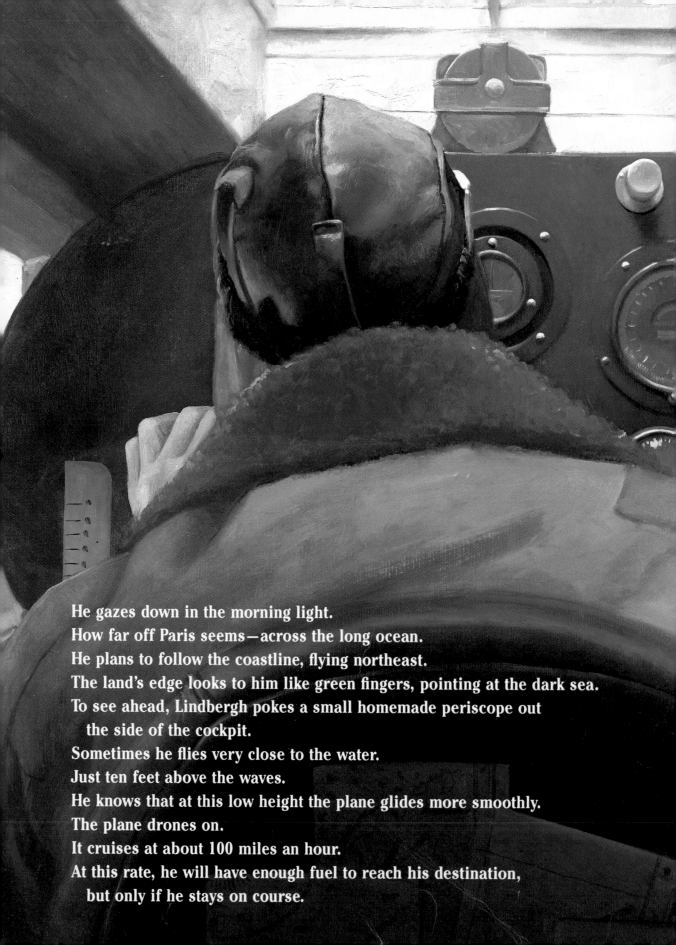

He gazes down in the morning light.
How far off Paris seems—across the long ocean.
He plans to follow the coastline, flying northeast.
The land's edge looks to him like green fingers, pointing at the dark sea.
To see ahead, Lindbergh pokes a small homemade periscope out
    the side of the cockpit.
Sometimes he flies very close to the water.
Just ten feet above the waves.
He knows that at this low height the plane glides more smoothly.
The plane drones on.
It cruises at about 100 miles an hour.
At this rate, he will have enough fuel to reach his destination,
    but only if he stays on course.

Beside him in the cockpit is a little book.
He keeps a diary as he goes: all day long, hour by hour.
It is as if he were speaking to himself.
He wants to remember everything.
Because no one else will ever really know.
At 12:08 he flies above Nova Scotia.
Just after 4:00 he flies above the coast of Newfoundland.
At dusk he looks down and sees icebergs!
In his diary he calls them "White pyramids . . .
White patches on a blackened sea; sentries of the Arctic."
He wonders what lies ahead.

The sun sets far behind the plane.
Lindbergh flies over St. John's, Newfoundland,
   the last point of land in North America.
Now he can no longer follow the land's edge for direction.
He must chart his course carefully.
The slightest movement could send him miles off course
   and risk the fuel supply.
He follows two compasses and the stars to navigate.
As long as the sky is clear, he is safe. But he must stay awake.
He writes: "Now I must cross not one, but two oceans:
One of night and one of water."
Time passes slowly.
It is almost 9:00 at night, Lindbergh's thirteenth hour in the air.
He has completed one-third of the flight.

He moves through dense, curling fog, lit ghostly white by the moon.

He suddenly enters a huge stormcloud.

The plane shimmers, moving up and down in the uniform blackness.

He wonders: Can I fly above it?

Slowly, he soars to 10,500 feet.

Here it is clear—but very, very cold.

He extends his arm outside the cockpit and feels "stinging pinpricks."

He clicks on his small flashlight and peers out:

Heavy ice has formed on the plane's wings.

He cannot risk his instruments' icing up.

He points the *Spirit of St. Louis* back down.

The wings quiver as they slice through the turbulent air.

The fog continues but now, at least, the air is warmer.

The ice begins to melt and Lindbergh roars ahead,
  through the fog and clouds, to Paris over 2,000 miles away.

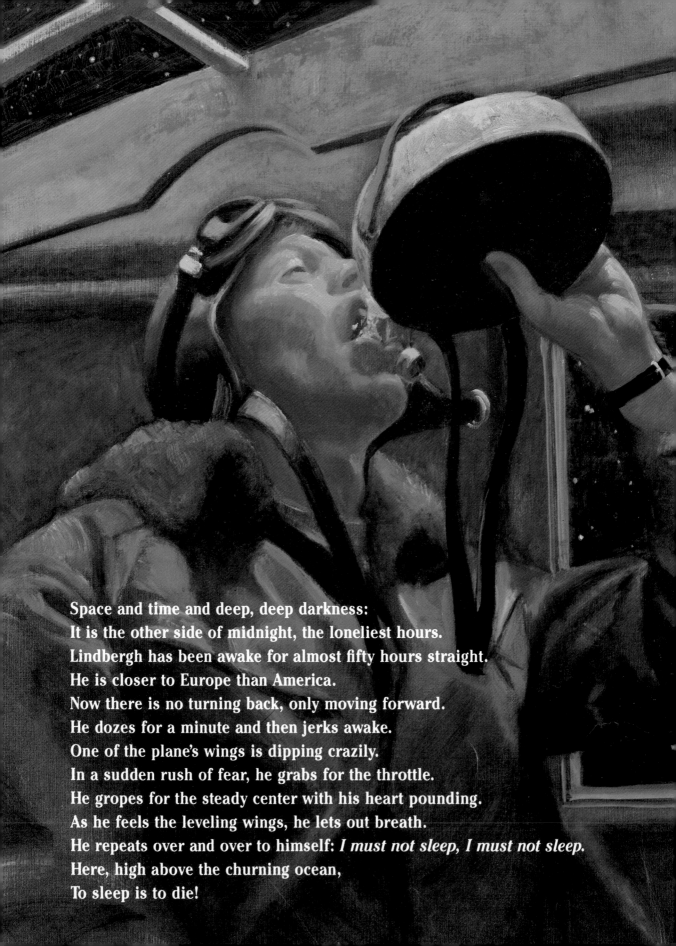

Space and time and deep, deep darkness:
It is the other side of midnight, the loneliest hours.
Lindbergh has been awake for almost fifty hours straight.
He is closer to Europe than America.
Now there is no turning back, only moving forward.
He dozes for a minute and then jerks awake.
One of the plane's wings is dipping crazily.
In a sudden rush of fear, he grabs for the throttle.
He gropes for the steady center with his heart pounding.
As he feels the leveling wings, he lets out breath.
He repeats over and over to himself: *I must not sleep, I must not sleep.*
Here, high above the churning ocean,
To sleep is to die!

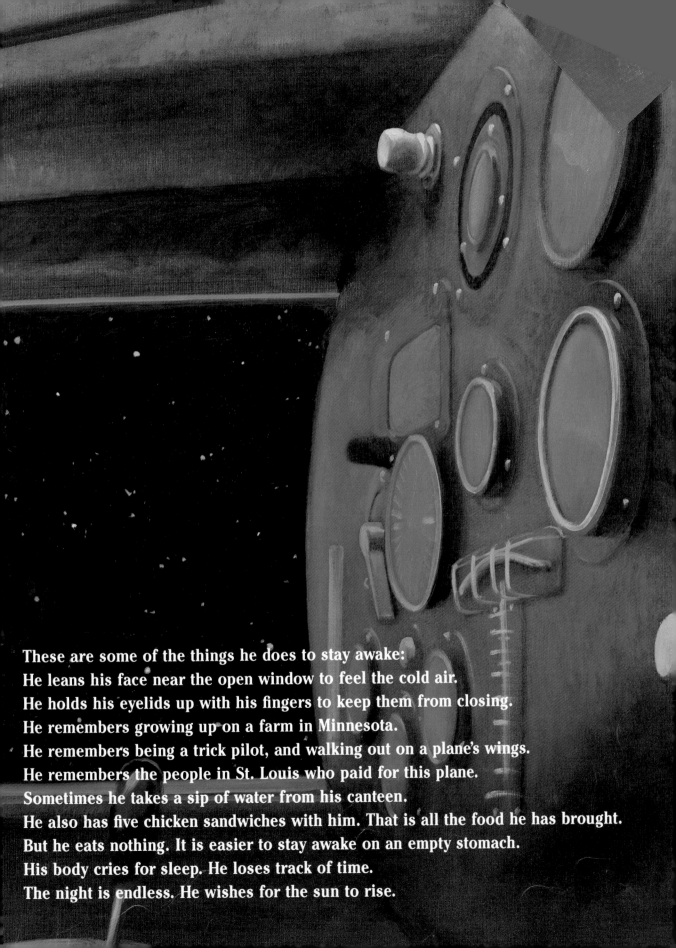

These are some of the things he does to stay awake:
He leans his face near the open window to feel the cold air.
He holds his eyelids up with his fingers to keep them from closing.
He remembers growing up on a farm in Minnesota.
He remembers being a trick pilot, and walking out on a plane's wings.
He remembers the people in St. Louis who paid for this plane.
Sometimes he takes a sip of water from his canteen.
He also has five chicken sandwiches with him. That is all the food he has brought.
But he eats nothing. It is easier to stay awake on an empty stomach.
His body cries for sleep. He loses track of time.
The night is endless. He wishes for the sun to rise.

Dawn comes slowly, growing out of the gray mist.

"Will the fog never end?" he wonders.

The clouds change color: "from green to gray, and from gray to red and gold."

Lindbergh has been in the air for twenty-three hours.

He is 2,300 miles from New York and has 1,300 miles to go.

He feels completely alone in the world.

He feels as if he were "flying through all eternity."

He tries to stay on course.

But because of his constantly curving route, he is not always sure.

Here and there, the clouds seem to break apart.

He sees, far below him, the ocean.

From high up it is like a great blue shaft, with gray walls.

Then he flies into the clouds again.

Into the unchanging mist.

The day comes on, brighter and warmer.
Sometimes he imagines he sees land.
No: it is only the flickering shapes of the clouds.
And water, water, water, endless water.
It is 7:30 in the morning in New York, and Paris is over a thousand miles away.
"There's no alternative but death and failure," he writes.
Flying closer to the water, Lindbergh sights a porpoise, leaping above the waves.
He spies a seagull.
Then fishing boats. Something quickens in Lindbergh's blood.
He guides the *Spirit of St. Louis* carefully down and down, to just above a boat.
He throttles the plane and calls out a question: "Which way," he shouts, "is Ireland
He hopes for a word. He longs for a wave,
". . . a warmer welcome back to the fellowship of men."
It is 10:52 in the morning, New York time.

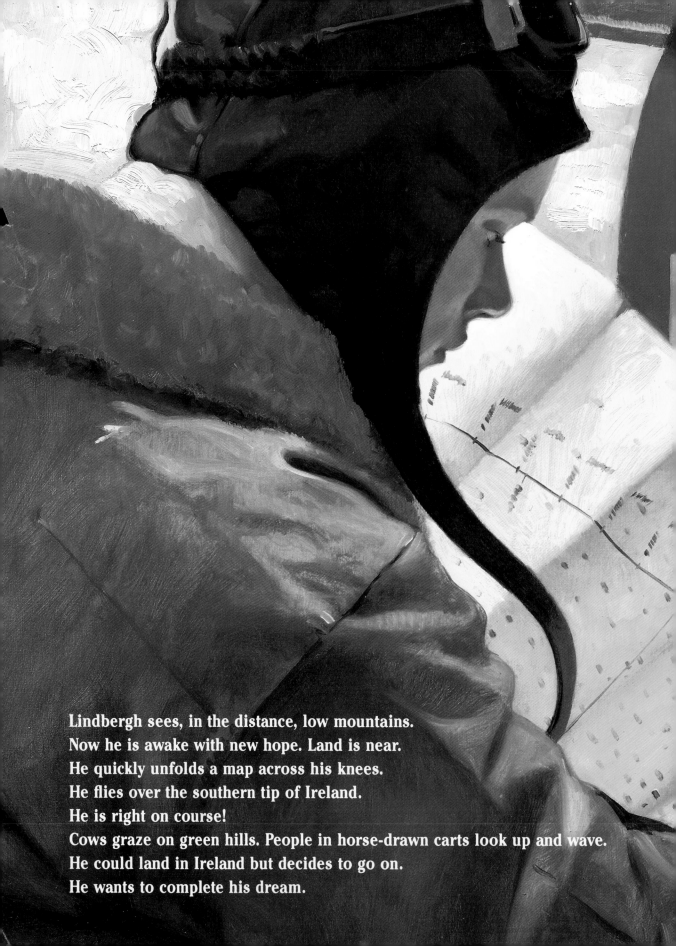

Lindbergh sees, in the distance, low mountains.
Now he is awake with new hope. Land is near.
He quickly unfolds a map across his knees.
He flies over the southern tip of Ireland.
He is right on course!
Cows graze on green hills. People in horse-drawn carts look up and wave.
He could land in Ireland but decides to go on.
He wants to complete his dream.

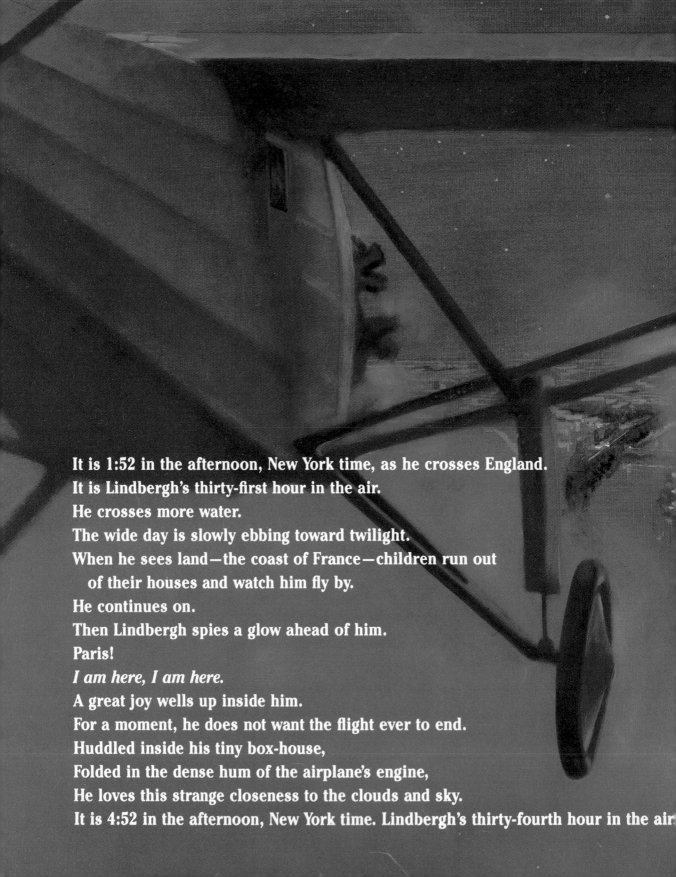

It is 1:52 in the afternoon, New York time, as he crosses England.
It is Lindbergh's thirty-first hour in the air.
He crosses more water.
The wide day is slowly ebbing toward twilight.
When he sees land—the coast of France—children run out
  of their houses and watch him fly by.
He continues on.
Then Lindbergh spies a glow ahead of him.
Paris!
I am here, I am here.
A great joy wells up inside him.
For a moment, he does not want the flight ever to end.
Huddled inside his tiny box-house,
Folded in the dense hum of the airplane's engine,
He loves this strange closeness to the clouds and sky.
It is 4:52 in the afternoon, New York time. Lindbergh's thirty-fourth hour in the air

From above, all Lindbergh sees are many, many small lights.
But now he must concentrate on just one thing: "the sod coming up to meet me."
Closer, closer, closer:
The plane touches the ground.
It bounces, rolls, hugs the solid earth.
It is 10:22, Paris time. The flight has taken thirty-three and a half hours.

Thousands of people are running toward the plane.
For a moment, Lindbergh is dazed.
It seems to him as if he were "drowning in a great sea."
People surround the plane, cheering.
But Lindbergh can hardly hear them.
His ears seem to have been deafened by the hours of roaring engine.
Crowds pull him out of the cockpit.
Men and women are calling his name, over and over.

They carry him on their shoulders.
Others begin to tear pieces of the plane.
More than anything else, Lindbergh wants to save the *Spirit of St. Louis.*
His first words are a question: "Are there any mechanics here?"
But no one speaks English.
Finally, two French aviators arrive to help him.
Policemen guard the plane.
The aviators take Lindbergh away from the still-cheering crowd.

In the airfield's hangar, he tells the story of his flight to the other pilots:
The cramped cockpit, the aloneness, the long, long night.
Meanwhile, unknown to Lindbergh, newspaper headlines
   all over the world are beginning to blazon the news:
AMERICAN HERO SAFE IN PARIS!
Lindbergh is driven off to the American Embassy.
He answers more questions about his flight.
He has not slept in over sixty hours.
Finally, at 4:15 in the morning he goes to bed.

When he wakes, his life will be changed forever.
When he wakes, there will be huge parades and medals and speeches.
He will be the most famous man in the world.
It is the year 1927.
It is 1927, and his name is Charles Lindbergh.